Memories of Kerry Life
in the 70s and early 80s
A. H. Vaughan

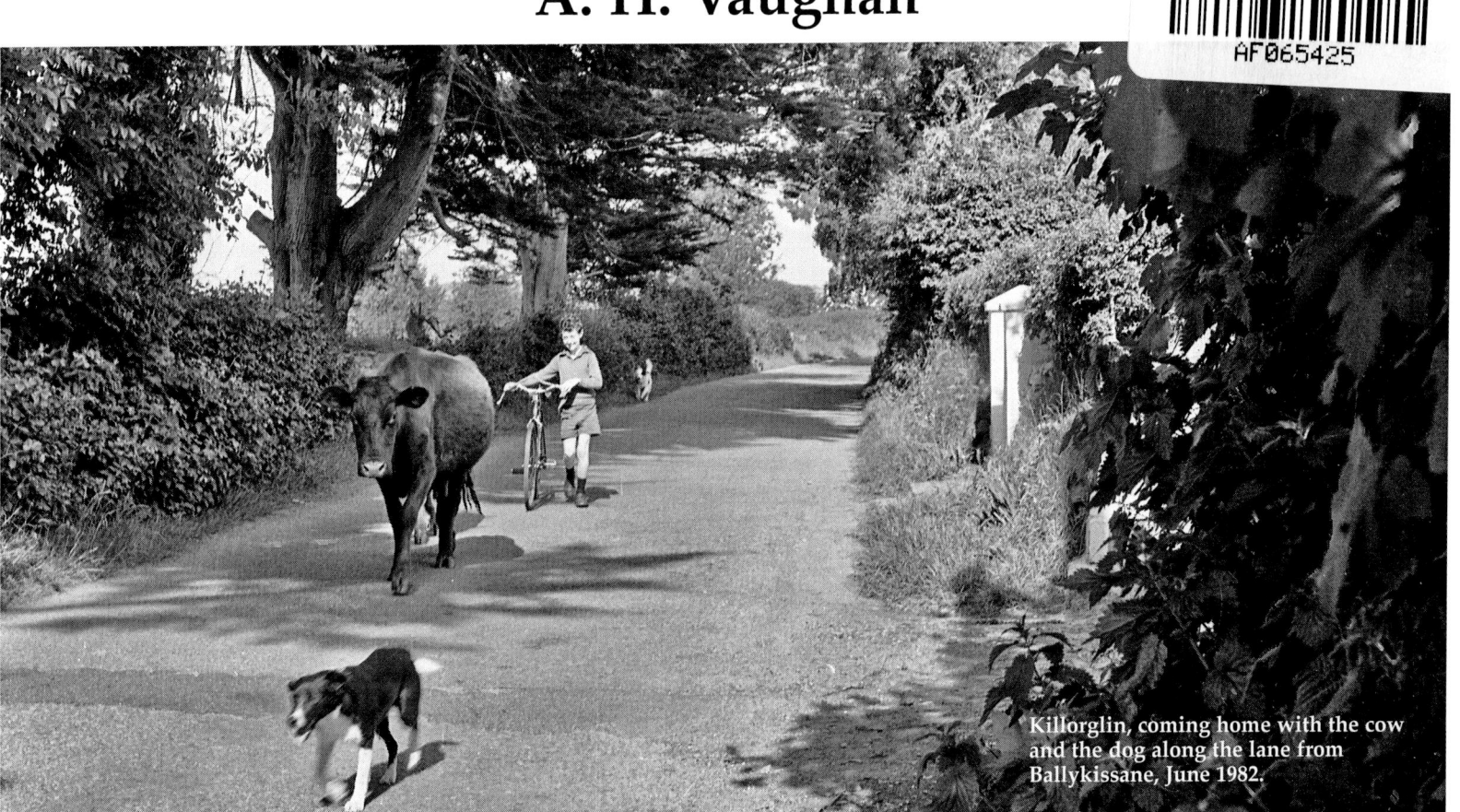

Killorglin, coming home with the cow and the dog along the lane from Ballykissane, June 1982.

© A. H. Vaughan, 2023
First published in the United Kingdom, 2023,
by Stenlake Publishing Ltd.
54-58 Mill Square,
Catrine, KA5 6RD
www.stenlake.co.uk
ISBN 978-1-84033-953-6

The publishers regret that they cannot supply copies of any pictures featured in this book.

Printed by
Blissetts, Unit E1-E8 Shield Drive,
West Cross Ind Pk, Brentford, TW8 9EX

Acknowledgements

I am very grateful for the help I received in naming streets and people. The Librarian at Tralee Library, Stephen Thompson of the Killorglin History Society, Gerard McMahon for Tralee streets, Joanne Tangney for her name and that of her sister at Firies, Pat Donovan for Kenmare.

Signpost at Gaddagh Bridge on one of the back roads from Killorglin to Beaufort, 23rd November 1981.

Introduction

I first came to Ireland in the summer of 1973 and was astonished at the relative poverty of the towns and villages comparing them with England. I had no idea of Ireland's history. I came with my wife, Susan, whom I married in 1972. Her father, John O'Sullivan, was a Kerry man whom I greatly admired. Since marrying I had tried to get a mortgage to buy a house, but my wages weren't enough. John suggested we go to Kerry where there were 'hundreds of abandoned cabins you could buy for what you've got in your pocket'. So in 1973 we went, we bought, and in 1975 we arrived at our derelict purchase. Our 1½ ton van parked, marking our arrival. We went through the gate and sat on the grass to rest after the journey and a few minutes later a grey Ferguson tractor stopped. The driver dismounted and came to the low wall bordering the road. He smiled, held out his hand to me and said, 'I'm Michael Doyle. I live up at the cross,' he said pointing along the road,' I'm pleased to see you both and if there's anything I can do to help, come up to my place and ask.'

I would not have been able to restore the cabin had not 'Chubb' Connor TD, owner of the Killorglin builders' yard been so generous with credit. The general friendliness from all around was happy. `We cut our share of turf on a bog rented by friends. Killorglin, the Beaufort road and Meanus West was part of a community of unpretentious, hard-working, people who owned their small businesses. The Laune River flowed wide out of the Killarney Lake past and around the town where the River Maine joined it into Dingle Bay, the Slieve Mish mountains flanking to the north and the Reeks to the south all the way to the great Atlantic Ocean. The land might have been a formidable place to live and farm and buy and sell, but these people who were friends to Susan and me, managed it. I came to love the Kerry and these are some of my photos of the place and the people.

Some of our many Kerry friends.
Upper left: Henry Dodd, May 1981.
Lower left: Eddie Moriarty & Rebecca, August 1980.
Upper right: Chubb Connor T.D. May 1981.
Lower right: Pat Clifford playing, August 1982.

Out of Abbeyfeale market place, Co. Limerick, 5th August 1977. The road curves south over the border into Kerry.

The road from Abbeyfeale arrives in the first town in Kerry, Castleisland. Looking to Knockane at the junction, July 1978.

Castleisland grocer and ice cream sales, 1973.

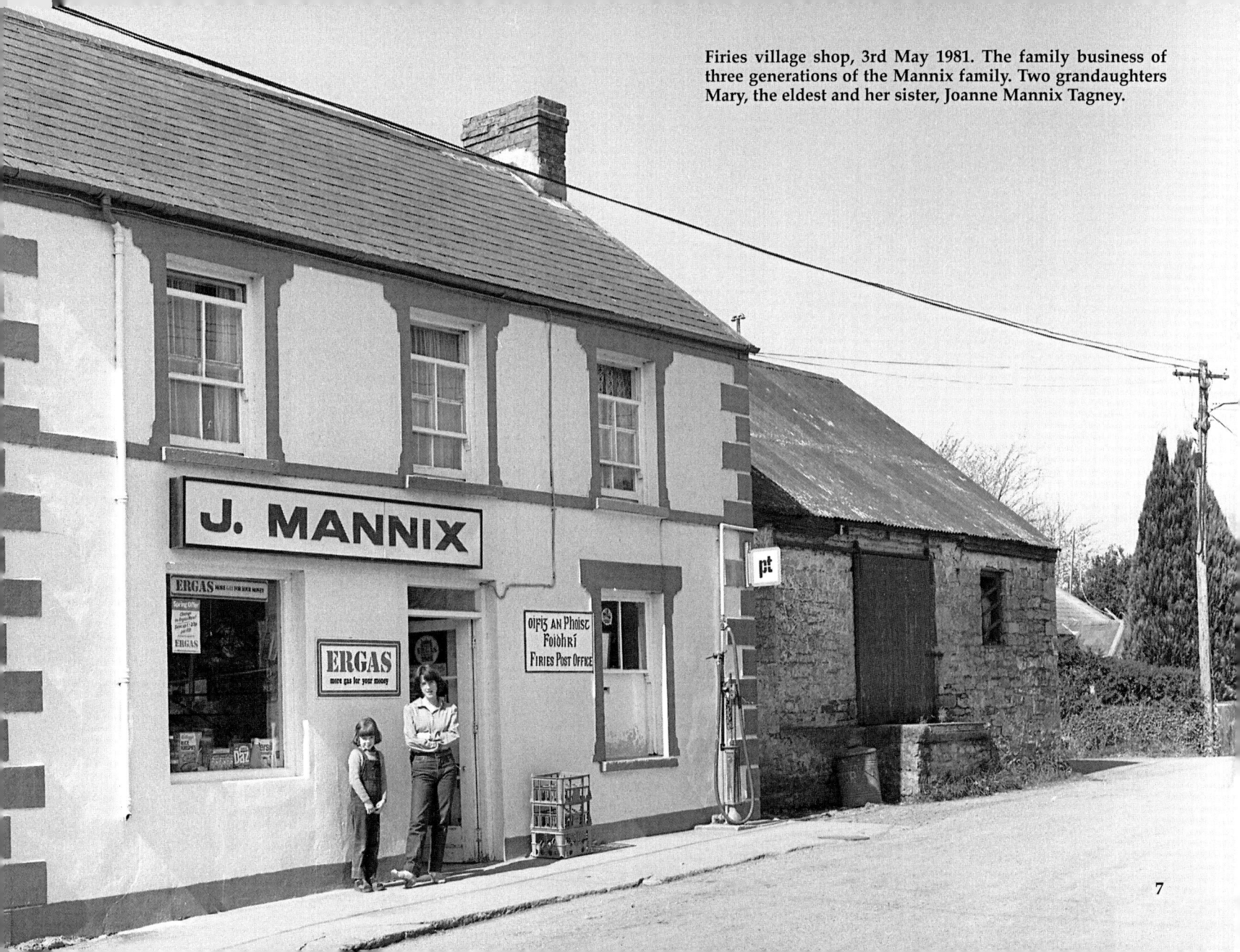

Firies village shop, 3rd May 1981. The family business of three generations of the Mannix family. Two grandaughters Mary, the eldest and her sister, Joanne Mannix Tagney.

Tralee, County town of Kerry, Denny Street, 4th August 1977. The monument honours the men who fought and died for Ireland in 1798. It also commemorates the risings of 1803, 1848 and 1867 and was unveiled on 6th June 1939.

Tralee, The Mall, Agust 1977.

Tralee, Russell Street, looking north from Bridge Street, August 1977.

Tralee, Bridge Street, looking east, March 1980.

Tralee, end of Bridge Street looking south, August 1977.

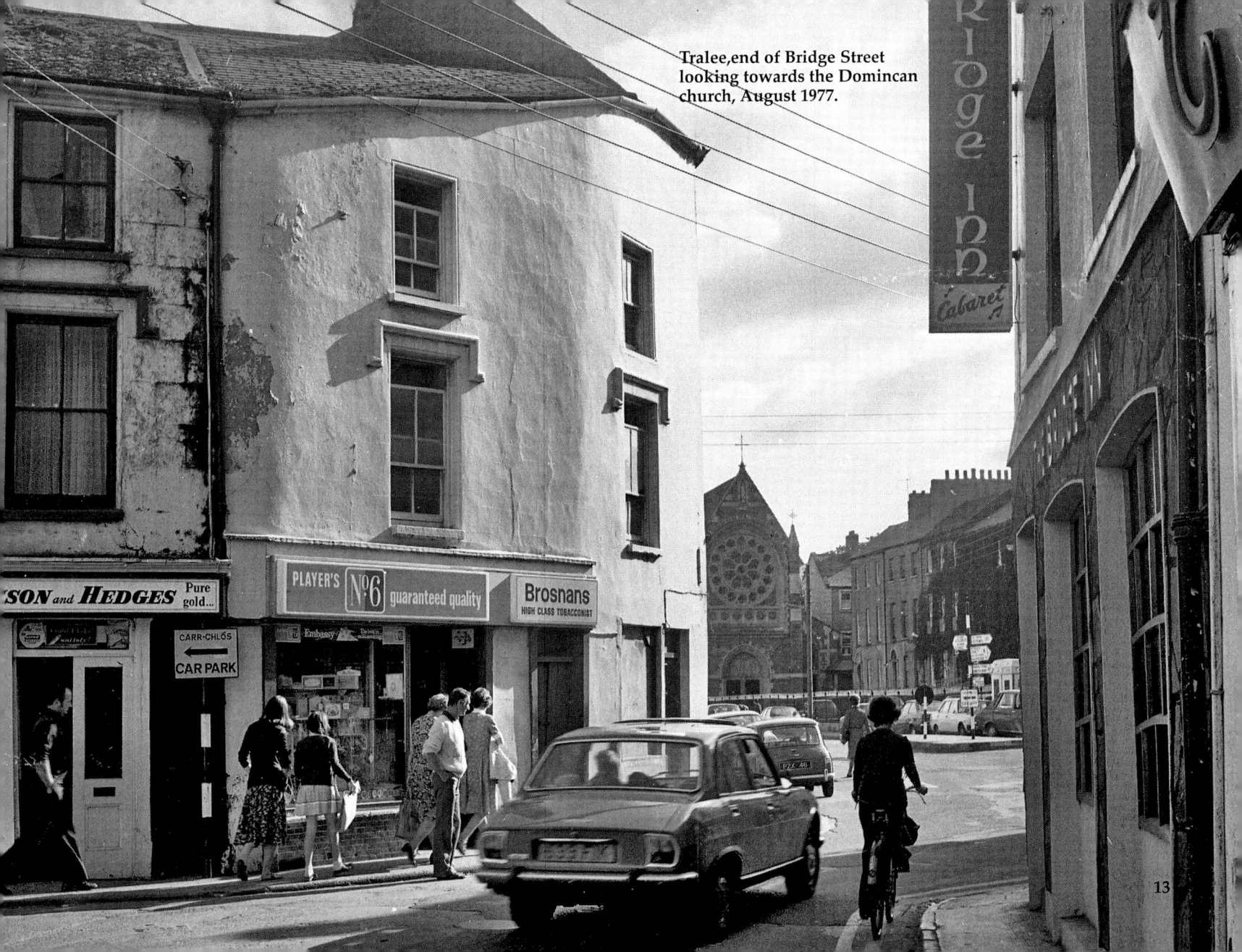

Tralee, end of Bridge Street looking towards the Domincan church, August 1977.

Tralee, Moyderwell looking to Upper Castle Street, August 1977.

Castlemaine, exit. Tralee left, Ballyfinane to the right, November 1982.

Castlemaine. Major junctions to famous places, November 1982. The ivy clad wall, on the right, is the remains of a mill.

Boolteens, along the Dingle road from Castlemaine. Florence O'Sullivan's forge and farrier workshop. Freddie the horse being shod while his owner, Timmy O'Shea is taking things easy. April 1979.

Boolteens. Florence O'Sullivan filing Freddie's hoof into shape. Florence retired from this work aged 88. A highly respected man. The village pub is named 'The Anvil' in his memory. The forge was often as great meeting place for the exchange of news as the pub.

Milltown refuse centre, August 1980. Never on the tourist trail, but an astonishing sight even so.

Killarney Main Street, looking north, 19th June 1977.
The road from Killorglin joins on the left.

Kenmare Main Street, 19th June 1977. The town stands above the River Roughty shortly upstream of where it widens into the ria flowing out to the Atlantic Ocean.

Kenmare Main Street looking to St. Patrick's Church, June 1977.

Kenmare Henry Street. I think the gentleman was searching anxiously for his wallet.

Gus surveys his 'estate', common land above the Kenmare River on the left, September 1976. He had all the mountains around to pasture his goats.

Killorglin town from Faill na Gahhair – the 'Cliff of Goats', 8th November 1978.

Killorglin, prize family outside Stevens & Champs shop. Mr. Champ in attendance, 1980. The prize bike and family inside the shop (*facing page*).

Killorglin, Mary McCarthy's shop and O'Sullivan's Bar, September 1979.

Mary inside her shop, September 1979.

There were many pubs in Killorglin but this was unique. Mrs. P.T O'Sullivan pulls a pint for Mr. Dye, August 1976.

Jimmy the Monk and Michael Doyle stand in the door of J J Foley's grocers, August 1976.

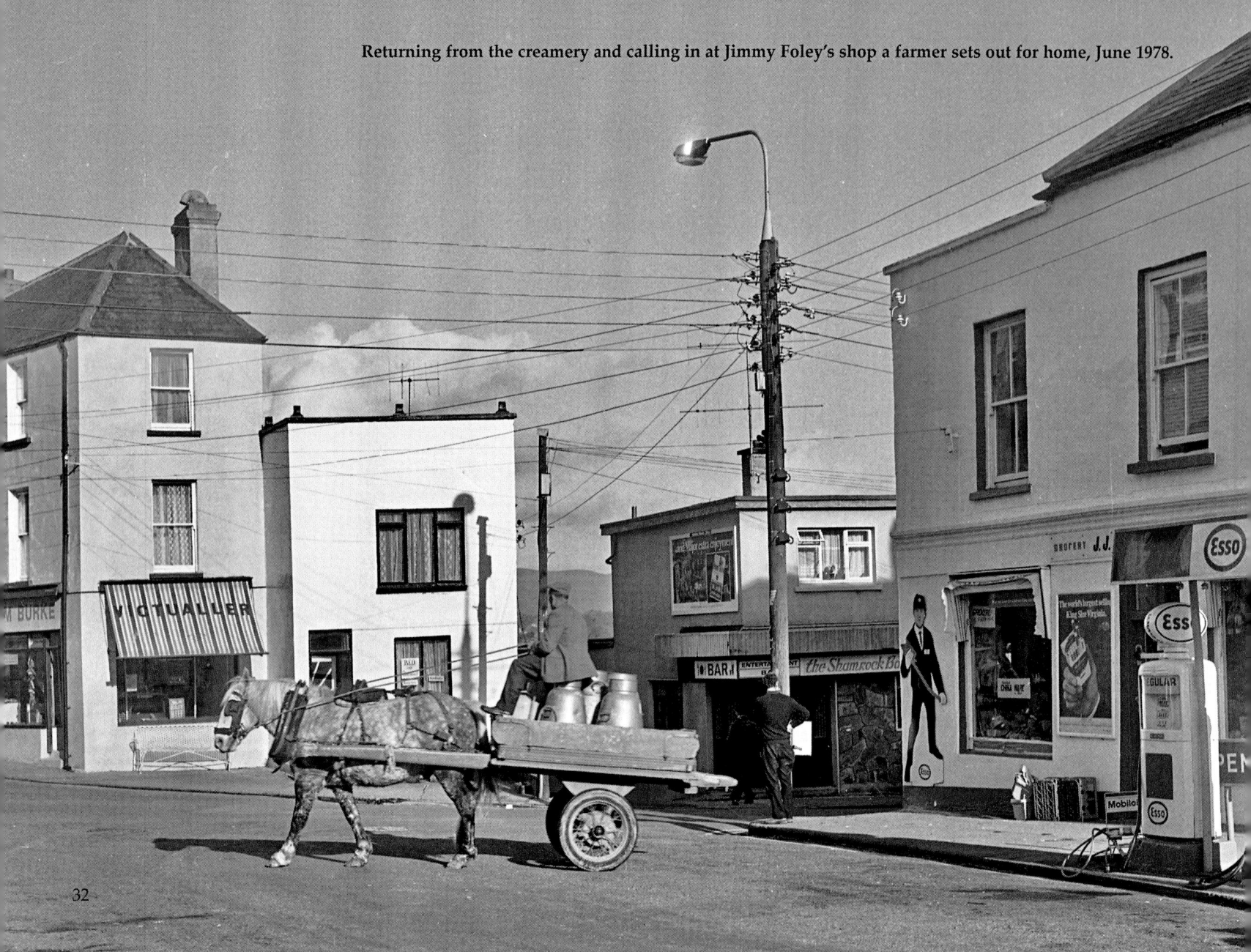

Returning from the creamery and calling in at Jimmy Foley's shop a farmer sets out for home, June 1978.

Dutch man selling vegetables and fish in Killorglin, 5th November 1982.

Killorglin, 20th November 1979 on the Iveragh road coming in from Caherciveen. Jack Foley's car repair garage next to Houlihan – there's nuthin' comes down but the ree-an, Ma'am – the butcher. At the far end Tom Melia's supermarket.

Killorglin, the May cattle and sheep fair: a messy business disliked by many shop owners, 1977.

Meanus West, near Killorglin, Brendan Kelly watches the sheep shearer at Eddie Moriarty's farm, 20th April 1982.

Cromane, the coastguard station as a pub, 27th April 1981. During the production of the 1970 film *Ryan's Daughter*, the Director, David Lean and Producer, Anthony Havelock-Allen went into Cromane Coastguard pub and heard the superb skill of fiddler Johnny Cahilane playing traditional Irish music. Johnny was recruited and he played his fiddle as background music for the film.

Cromane. Mechanical threshing machine at work, 20th September 1980.

Cromane. Con Cahilane and John McCarthy feeding the machine.

Cromane. Boys after school taking up a fishing net at low tide in Dingle Bay, 20th September 1980. The Slieve Mish mountains to the north.

Cromane, O'Riordan's shop, 20th September 1980.

Kerryman who stopped to talk on the road to Caherciveen.

Mountain Stage. Riordan's shop, 13th April 1979. I photographed from the wide space where the railway station once had been.

Caherciveen from Top Street, 1980.

Cahersiveen Quay, March 1980, lobster pots a reminder of the long history of trawlers – *Pato's Wish*, *Sancta Lucia* and hundreds of others worked by Caherciveen men out on the great ocean.

Leaving Portmagee, 30th June 2006, for the great pinnacle of rock that is Skellig Michael, ten miles out into the Atlantic, a ragged, jagged rock rising 754 feet above the ocean.

Standing off Skelllig Michael while another Portmagee boat's passengers climb up onto the footpath.

The 'beehive huts are domed and erected without mortar – dry stone work at its best. They were built by Irish Christian monks, hermits, in the 7th century, hoping to please God and save their souls for eternity.